Also by T.S. SIMMONS
when the secret hour of pleasure nears

The Bleeding Angels

T.S. SIMMONS

With photographs by Gregory Varano

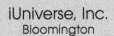

iUniverse, Inc.
Bloomington

The Bleeding Angels

iUniverse books may be ordered through booksellers or by contacting:

iUniverse
1663 Liberty Drive
Bloomington, IN 47403
www.iuniverse.com
1-800-Authors (1-800-288-4677)

Because of the dynamic nature of the Internet, any web addresses or links contained in this book may have changed since publication and may no longer be valid. The views expressed in this work are solely those of the author and do not necessarily reflect the views of the publisher, and the publisher hereby disclaims any responsibility for them.

The model depicted in this edition was provided by Gregory Varano Artist/Photojournalist, and such images are being used for illustrative purposes only. Unauthorized use, copy, display, or distribution of any photograph taken by Gregory Varano is strictly prohibited. You do not have permission to use these photos in any form without the written consent of Gregory Varano Artist/Photojournalist.

All photographs Copyright © Gregory Varano Artist/Photojournalist (except where noted).

Photo on page 65 appears courtesy of Truc Chau and T.S. Simmons.

Photographer's Note: All images were taken with the Leica M8 Camera and a 50mm F2 Summicon lens.

ဢ Designed by Truc Chau ര

ISBN: 978-1-4759-9065-2 (sc)
ISBN: 978-1-4759-9066-9 (ebk)

Library of Congress Control Number: 2013908755

Printed in the United States of America

iUniverse rev. date: 05/20/2013

❧⚬☙

With love to
the bleeding angel
who whispered
"Come to me..."
10.02.09

❧⚬☙

The Bleeding Angels

Contenta in eodem

ಹಿಂ

"Life is a journey.
Death is a return to earth.
The universe is like an inn.
The passing years are like dust.

Regard this phantom world
As a star at dawn, a bubble in a stream,
A flash of lightning in a summer cloud,
A flickering lamp - a phantom - and a dream."

Buddha

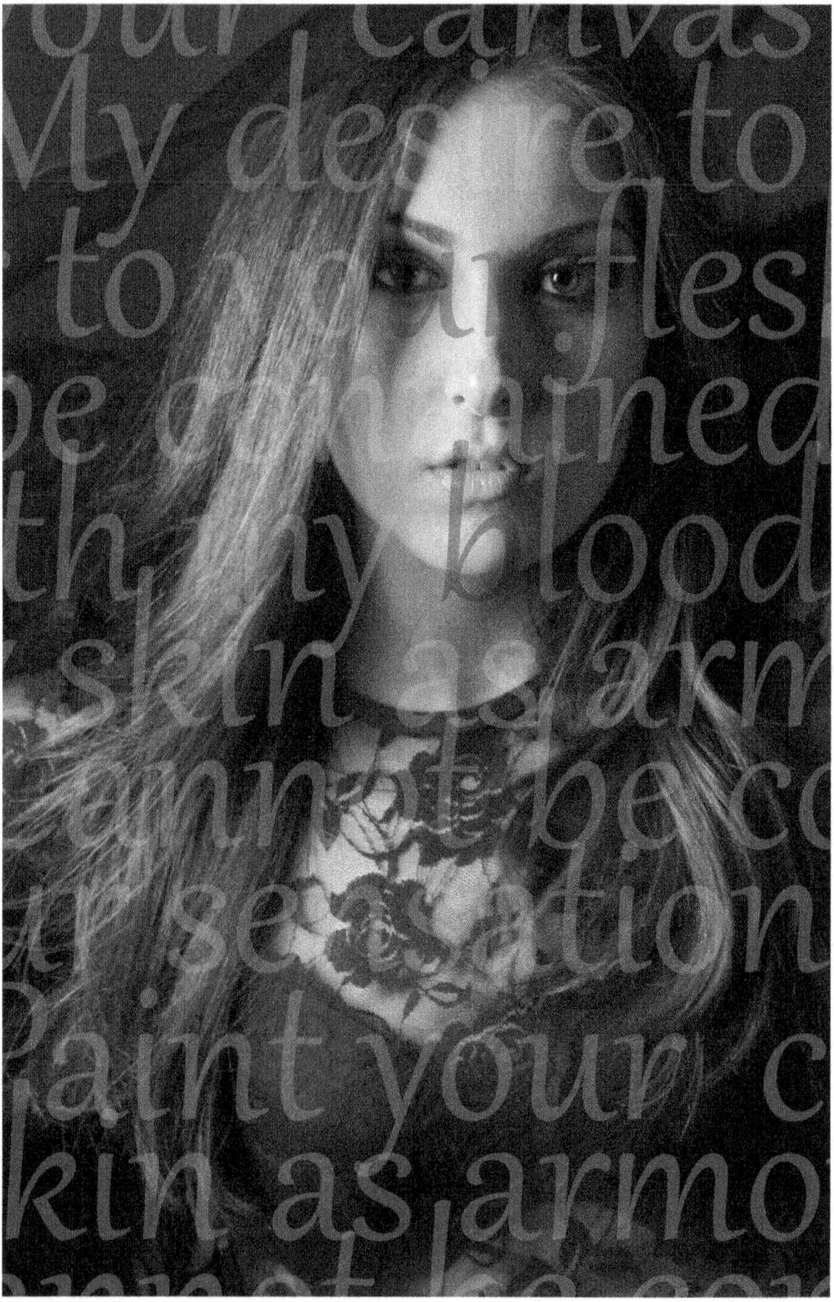

She Comes at Night

She comes at night
through rain distraught and weeping
down upon her jangling silver anklet
and each burning drop
screams with grief in the visions
of offering such a lover
to the glowing urban nightmare

Though somewhere
a piano mourns gently
my wineglass bleeding on the floor
as I slouch toward consciousness
in decaying flower exhalations

While her jeweled shoes
hold sad commuters captive
her damp splendid hair testifies
to her wild rejection of sanity
as she flows like death
to see me

When I Awakened To You

In May, I supposed
that if I touched your hair
I would never again dissent to
the toll of the clock tower
in midnight suffering

I watched you and
cried for your beauty
those nights I spent alone
staring from illuminated windows
in search of recollection

You whispered that
we each wore masks to

shield our hearts and
laid your face upon my shoulder
and the twilight coveted your lips

You sang in anguish
for the changing seasons
and we shared the sadness
like wine
upon the grass behind
the faded hotel
where you were distressed
about crushing the
flowers

On Her Birthday She is Missing and the Night Hopes To Devour Me

As the night opened
her ritual oyster
and the sky rained her
sacrificial baptism
upon me
the street wept
finding its ritual infant
laid in offering
at your feet

There was nothing so hopeless
as your empty apartment
so ashen with solitude
the Umeshu bottle
in your white kitchen

casting me to the mourning atrium
a limping invalid

Though I was later to
kneel upon your floor
I now offer you my gratitude
for when I kissed you
in the glow of the streetlight
you responded in kind
and did not retreat
from my breath of wine
nor my lips
wet with the blood of purgatory
Not once speaking of
our fragmented hearts

For CM

Glorious artist and child of sun I
stopped to see his face, burning
and shrouded with wisps of hair not
obscuring his vision. Torrid etchings of
life upon the blanched nature of flesh
spoke and listened and dreamed within
bounds that did not hold him at all
O did there exist a truer artist in
this realm struggling with decay in
words and refusing to be held by
the chains of confinement and confusion
He sought truth and beauty in each
passing moment each flicker of time and death
though himself scarred with markings of
greatness his imagination will free him
forever.

The Artist, Condemned

Paint your canvas with my blood
Take my skin as armor to your flesh
My desire to live within your sensation
cannot be contained
I resign myself to sweet hypnosis
in the sanctuary of your eyes
with your perfumed skin
to nourish me
and your breath tasting of desires
encountered only within
the obscurity of dream
as I feel your fingers burn
an exotic dance upon me
I know you shall condemn me
To suffer in ecstasy

Burnout

In this cryptic lighting
so favored by lovers
I contemplate the death of silence
slain unceremoniously
by the complexities
that my escort wields

While retaining their opulence
her lips taste of poison
the night is incised by her stare
and must fall in identical pieces
to lay in broken sanctum
at my feet

In this feast of violence
my lover shares her revelation
relegates to me a title: *burnout*
I respond benevolently
telling her something I had heard
"To burn-out, you must first be on fire"

As such, her indication to depart
is clothed stylishly in outrage
Though when I rise to
bid her farewell
I swear I see the glowing cinders
rising from my body

La Bohème Francaise

That day I saw her
was, in reality a moment
Her hair fell in oceans, as if
she had been baptized in beauty
the remnants to ceaselessly frame her
in soft wet ringlets
they rested in ferocity
upon her scarf
tied like an orphan girl
from the bohemian quarter

I could not look into her eyes
for fear of drowning
though I walked the shore of her presence
and followed the horizon of her artful gait

She wore soldier's boots, laced high
and feathers
rested gently in her ears to
dance upon skin, the
color of a seashell I once had found
as a lonely child

Then, with feigned apathy
I stared, enraptured
as she plucked tobacco
from her worn pouch
and rolled a cigarette
with a delicate passion
Like she was caressing
her lover

Sensuality's Voyeur

The girl at the intersection of
Rue de Medicis and
Boulevard Saint-Michel
shuffles her worn brown shoes
on the decaying curb
as the clock strikes six and
cries desolately
along a city passage
as empty as a soul
and she is one with the sublime
though it must be said that
all French women
are resonant with such beauty
to make a G-dless man fall to his knees
in prayer

O my drunken brother
in your silent knowledge
beneath the earth of Montparnasse
I carry my fouled attendance
in search of you
Stumbling upon the dying flowers
of Simone and Sartre
their branched arms reach to me in offering

Au croisement de la
Rue de Médicis et
du Boulevard Saint-Michel
la jeune fille traîne ses souliers marron
sur le trottoir délabré
alors que l'horloge sonne 6 coups
comme des pleurs de désespoir
le long de l'allée aussi
vide qu'une âme
elle ne fait qu'un avec le sublime
à l'image de toute
femme française
vibrante de cette beauté
qui fait tomber le plus athée des hommes
en prière

Mon frère d'ivresse
dans ton savoir silencieux
sous la surface de Montparnasse
Je supporte ma présence souillée
à ta recherche
Et trébuche sur les fleurs mortes
de Simone et Sartre
leurs bras tendus vers moi en offrande

Sensuelle et Voyeuriste

a penny for this shattered existential
yet in my vision streaked with infirmity
I seek you elsewhere
but not in the spindled cocoon of death
that is not you but, resembles me
as I am soon to rest upon you in my gratitude
beneath the mocking sun

You shall remain the frayed saint of wisdom
She to become one with the mementos of night
I feel her in the blessed air
now partially secluded beneath the cloisters
she consecrates all envy and desire upon us
with a single stir of her fragile body
and one hand to the corner of her flushed lips
what grail of perfection she seeks
has been found in my private hallucinations of her
as existent as the chaliced blood
resting beside my worn book of poems
I would open it to find her
if there she did not stand
sweet and superbly unaware of my presence
Sensuality's voyeur

d'un centime pour cette existence anéantie
or malgré ma vision abîmée par son infirmité
Je te cherche ailleurs
mais pas dans l'enveloppe de bois mortuaire
qui n'est pas toi mais me ressemble
bientôt c'est sur toi que je reposerais avec gratitude
sous le soleil narquois

Tu te dois de demeurer le saint aux frontières de la sagesse
Elle se doit de devenir le souvenir ineffable de la nuit
Je la sens dans l'air bénis
à présent en partie retirée derrière les cloîtres
son envie et désir nous sont entièrement consacrés
en un seul mouvement de son corps fragile
en une seule main au coin de ses lèvres vermeilles
sa quête de perfection
J'ai retrouvé dans l'une de mes hallucinations intimes d'elle
aussi vivante que le sang sacré
qui siège près de mon livre usé de poèmes
Je l'ouvrirais pour la trouver
si elle ne se tenait pas là
douce et superbement inconsciente de ma présence
Sensuelle et voyeuriste

Sensuelle et Voyeuriste

June 6, 1989

To carry the bones of death
I had burned my spirit in fire
and darkened my face
with the ashes
of warfare

When in the strangeness
born of discontent
I heard the trees awaken
to wear the season
flourished on their breasts

In my confused presence
beneath the maiden of solstice
I searched for reason and
found the void

Yet I was not aware
of the blessing in that moment
as the Lotus
laid her sad eyes
upon the northern landscape
Piercing it
with her eastern beauty

Two Angels as I Paint

Coltrane surges
from my ancient radio
Gitanes and empty jade bottles
have bled their loneliness dry

The earth is dying
The night avenges
and crickets
sing in terror

Appease,
and perhaps we shall
not be destroyed
Though we will
anyway

Tonight my shirt is torn,
my expression as peaceful
as Maudit, the angel on his bed
carried by his friends
to immortality

And I am alone, thinking that
I want to smash the mirrors
to thrust the shards into my flesh
to adorn the canvas with my veins

The weight of centuries
hangs within the dust
and Juliet turns tricks
for her entourage

I'm thinking
about her lips
this very moment
and I loathe
my fragile heart

Though,

When I touch the
reflections of sorrow

in my paintings of you
I am released from
the famines of the night

As your mouth returns
to nourish me, I am one
with your unadorned flesh
and wish to sleep within
the wild storms of your hair
Lost within the faith of passion

A Divine Surrender

Lay yourself upon the night
as sacred as these lotus fields
and I will celebrate your splendor
I will rejoice in your eyes

Spin the knives of paradise
Illuminate my visions
Let me suffer in the reflections
carried upon your wings

Though your blush may enter nightfall
hurried as a stranger
I will bow before your hidden form
a divine surrender

Messenger

And when I depart, I feel you
on the surface of my skin
like the lotus effect
holds the rain to water leaves
I continue to touch you
even as your presence recedes

I have seen this
in my moonlit visions
What can they tell me
about your passion
that I do not know?

In the spiritual atheism
of my acquainted isolation

I resist all exorcism of you
I long for your sweet toxin
to govern my veins
and possess my spirit
to your breast

As today, I look upon a tree
you once had spoken to
with your eyes alone
I have carved its response
into my own memory
and shall carry it
to inform you
with my lips

Strangely Spiritual

And I saw myself distorted in veneration
as your occurrence poured the interval of
the room up to the murky skylight
and those evening fires
danced upon your lips

While the books of the divine
offer mournful dust in arched corners
their phrasing is traumatized
with mould and decay
as even death speaks softly in your presence

You hold the secret knowledge
of my tarnished sanities
and their healing violence
Yes, there within your whisper
you acknowledge my own fatalities

Here in this fetid chamber
as the profane shall toast their empty adulations
I alone shall fall in confession to your beauty
for tonight you have left me feeling
strangely spiritual

September 23rd

Three bottles of
Cotes du Rhone
and who knows
what else
ingested like the night

In one swallow of darkness
the psychedelic lights were
dancing upon my skin

As jazz bled from
every corner of the room
running over my lips and
down to my chest and
drenching me in dream

or nightmare
I'm never sure
of which

As the fires of dawn
filtered through
stainless steel blinds
to burn
my funeral suit
and leave me naked
with the Water Nymph
of Nysa
holding my head
as if I was her
injured child

I Was Dying Until She Whispered...

With her movement a celestial sculpture
unrivaled in its formless art
I pursued the flow of her porcelain hands
and in that confusion of sound and light
I was as a child weeping quietly in awe
beneath the vaulted layers of heaven

I desire to unravel the silent beauty of her existence
to fall blindly into her fading silhouette
to hear her naked sensuality sigh to me
and fall in searing breaths upon my skin
as I rescind the entirety of my faith at her feet
Is she aware of her mystic engagement?

Dying Orpheus, I am one with her illusion
my spirit fades into her presence
there among the leaves and white blossoms
to be awakened from my sweetest death
beneath the halogen burn of the hotel ceiling
as she whispers, "Hoyas are like perfect stars"

December's Angel

And there, in the December night, stood beauty. The wind roared like death and music rose from the sidewalk tomb. Her body, like a ghost of whispered passion, touched my hand and I bowed as she danced without movement, on the empty street.

Was she real? Was I?

Amid this dream in progress, I noticed the timid splendor in her glance, and I shuddered and cried and kissed the darkness in ecstasy. I fell into the lap of this flower in the midnight strewn city. I lifted her, and her spirit soared and I chased her sacred presence into the night.

She thought I was watching the moon, but how could I?

With the snowfall wet in her hair.

I Once Drank White Wine
with an Angel

I once drank white wine
with an angel
When you look at me, I know
it is difficult to believe
though it is true
and
I must tell you that
one always imagines
encounters with
the divine and
the presence
of exaltedness
with immense fear
and
I was among
the terrified

However
I must tell you
that I knew all fear
to be unwarranted
when she smiled
with me
not upon me
without ceremony
folding her wings
(they were black)
under her hair
(also black)
as I thought
that previous
to this encounter
I was virginal

to the beauty of an experience
I can only describe as
an embrace
in soft rain

Then suddenly
she was profound and
intensely humorous
Did you expect angels
to be humored?
I did not
I laughed with her
and touched my own tears
as we were watched
by one thousand
yellow eyes
not one of which was

my old friend death
for he surrendered
to her light
I, too surrendered
though in a different form
She knew this

And now, as locusts feed
upon my flesh, as
the legions of Sonneillon contend
to hold my heart, as
the earth is wrought
in seething plague
I resist all suffering
You see,
I once drank white wine
With an angel

Can I Borrow Some Ecstasy? (She asked)

It has been said that
I have a superior memory
though I struggle to remember
blood
framed by my existence
and burning in my veins
as it did on the day
I took my seat beside
the angel of sadness

I reached for her hand
in the desolate marina
where the planks were damaged and
beauty seeped from the fractures
Or was it from our own?

She fed me chocolate
and whispered that the water
was laid in diamond wreaths

I was in concurrence
observing the ballet of her eyelashes
upon the ancient depth of her eyes

The worn wooden bench
held me and
I became one
with everything
As she threw open her shirt
to expose her breasts
to the sun
and whispered
Can

I

borrow

some

ecstasy

?

Why Can I Surrender
To Sleep in Your Arms?

Once I held death my lover
and breathed her violet plume
as the bloodless face of dawn
shone to liberate me
from the poisons of desire
I observed the street,
entombed in silence

Could it be that you were there?
No.

I searched bravely for you
in that corridor painted
with the glow of insanity
watching and waiting
ever lonely in my heroic quest

Later, battered with daylight
I decayed in the café
still looking for you

Then the rain began, and
the waitress didn't like the naked woman
on the cover of my book
she told me with her eyes, her
mouth sewn like a muted corpse

I should have been afraid
but I could feel you touch me
from the window of your apartment
and something changed within me
I noted the pale, dying stars, the
abject terror of the euthanized moon
and was woven with valour

Anything else? (The waitress asked)

Yes, I said
A spirit has embraced me,
in the context of anarchy

and I am still overcome
with the beauty of that moment

The waitress disappeared quickly,
and whispered into the
sunken-eyes of the manager
something about a 'drunk'

I smiled, for intoxication
is a flower of countless blooms
and walked outside, decreed by the sky
the sun now brooding in its ruin

I drew the perfumed breaths of gratitude
as your spirit could not be uncovered
for it bled enraptured from my pores
lifting me within its sweet invocations
to surrender to sleep in your arms

Mortality

Sprawled peacefully
a renaissance sculpture
upon the asphalt
when they towed the modern art
that was his car
it didn't fit with the décor
though now
clad in his very own
coroner's shawl
he did not seem concerned with
aesthetics
as the palette of his blood
was painted from the scene
I passed serenely
in shared humanity
and wondered
what he had
worried about
that morning

The Drowning

The night fell blue upon my shoulders
advising me in sad whispers of her absence
I replied within the silence of my breath
alone in the darkened passage where I had once
kissed the soft electricity of the angel's flesh

Sister hope stood smoking quietly in the doorway
turning from me as if she were a stranger
I stopped to read the expression on her face
and discovered that she was well prepared
for her sabbatical of indifference

I fell from the shielding beauty of the angel's womb
renounced upon the stained platform of darkness
the pieces of her spirit vanished through my fingers

I struggled to enclose them within my fragile hands
but weakness grew to surround me

As the trees bleeding leaves into the street
sang their weeping lyric to the sky
they inflicted the blindness of abandon
upon the shadow of their eyes
and I fell in surrender to death

Beyond this city's tangled desolation
oceans rose and fell in infinite birth
they held faith above the ruins of supremacy
but I was not to be salvaged with her light
for my heart drowned in Atlantis

In the Madness That Was

She lived on
the top floor of a hotel
I rode the elevator
in the evenings, hoping to
experience her beauty

We would lie naked
on her red shag carpet
as the hypnotic night
edged the intensity
of her body

I thought she was
an apparition, that
I only existed

within the realm of
her haunted eyes

Then
she whispered
"Are you alive?"
I could feel her breath burning
on the surface of my skin

"Yes" I said
and so we were alive, together
in that city of madness
in that season of loss
I wanted to
inhabit her presence
forever

I am Nothing and Everything

She said I am the sun
love me
or I shall burn you
I was motionless
and burned

She said I am the moon
fall before me
or you shall drown in the tide
I was confused
and drowned

She said I am the sky
kneel before my majesty
or I shall suffocate you
I was angered
and suffocated

She said I am God
worship me
or I shall destroy you
it was then I laughed
for I was God

Elegy

Ephemeral child, scented with orange blossom
I hold an elegy upon my lips for you tonight
for you are unaware of my secret baptism
In the flourish of your descending hair
as you leaned to dance, and your laughter
anointed me in spiritual armor
Sweet guardian, you shall rise
against the revelries of madness
though none may possess you
I am to fall into your arms, as
Signorelli's angels
To rest in your
Wild
Desire

The Bleeding Angels

T.S. Simmons Acknowledges

ဆာ

Truc Chau (Editor, Designer, and Publicist) for love, moral guardianship, and for tirelessly editing the insanity of my words into flowing ink, creating this dark beautiful tapestry all on your own. Without you, this book would not have been possible. The soul of your artistry knows no bounds.

Gregory Varano (Photographer) for the darkness of your vision, and your resolute direction.

Jessica Petrozza (Model) for your professionalism, form, and humor amid the grueling intensity of the shoots.

Desi Varano (Makeup Artist) for your creativity. Your work is transformative.

Marie Delmaire (Translator) for translating my words into le langage de l'amour.

Gregory Varano Acknowledges

ဆာ

Thanks TS for the opportunity, Jessica you are an Angel and Desi for your unwavering love and support.

T.S. Simmons...

Gregory Varano is an award-winning photographer who resides in Stouffville, Ontario, Canada. Varano has worked for many English and Italian publications in Canada, The United States and Europe. Varano's audience know him for his classic black and white style and photojournalistic approach. Varano has won acclaim for his cinematic "film noir" vision to his subject matter.

Also by T.S. SIMMONS

ഊൽ

when the secret hour
of pleasure nears

the poetry of T.S. Simmons
with photographs by Cameron MacMaster